FLASH POINTS

POWER ON!
LIFE-CHANGING TECHNOLOGY

Eleanor Cardell

Power On!
Flash Points

Full Tilt Press
42982 Osgood Road
Fremont, CA 94539
readfulltilt.com

Full Tilt Press publications may be purchased for educational, business, or sales promotional use.

Design and layout by Sara Radka
Copyedited by Renae Gilles

Alamy: Jens Wolf, 26, 25, 29; Getty Images: 6, 9, 21, 32, 33, David Paul Morris, 36, David Paul Morris, 37, Ethan Miller, 31, iStockphoto, 48, Justin Sullivan, 37, 39, Patrik Stollarz, 38, Peter Macdiarmid, 28; Newscom: 15, The Print Collector/Heritage-Images, 5, Newscom, ZUMAPRESS/Jack Kurtz, 35, Shutterstock, 7 (top), 7 (bottom), 11, 12, 17 (top), 17 (bottom), 30, 32, 36, 43: Anna Hoychuk, 42, Bloomicon, 41, Everett Historical, 16, 23, Keith Homan, 27, Tinxi, 26, 27, wantanddo, 22, ymgerman, 40; Wikimedia:, 6, 8, 12, 16, 19, 20, 23, 42

ISBN: 978-1-62920-607-3 (library binding)
ISBN: 978-1-62920-619-6 (eBook)

Contents

The Telephone

March 10, 1876

Alexander Graham Bell sits quietly at his desk in a busy machine shop. He is focused on a small toy-like machine made of metal and wood. He has finally finished building his telephone. He spent years trying to get it right. He tried hundreds of different designs. Now he is ready to test it.

Bell ignores the sounds of other workers around him. Metal clangs. Wood creaks. Electricity hums. Bell puts his face against the wooden top of the device. He speaks into his telephone.

"Mr. Watson, come here. I want to see you."

Bell's chair creaks as he leans back. Moments later, he hears footsteps pounding up the stairway outside the lab. His assistant, Thomas A. Watson, bursts in. Watson has just run up three flights of stairs. He had been sitting at a similar device, a long wire connecting the two. Watson's face is flushed. His breathing is loud. He cries, "I can hear you! I can hear the words!"

Bell has just made the first telephone call.

The first telephones were so big and heavy they had to be mounted on a wall or put on a sturdy table.

DID YOU KNOW?
One of Bell's very first telephone designs used an actual ear from a dead body.

How and Why

The creation and use of new technology is a process. Many different people, events, and ideas come together when new technology is needed. Below are some things that led to Bell's invention of the telephone.

An Old Idea

People had been trying to send messages across great distances for hundreds of years. There are records of people trying many different devices since the 1600s. But early machines couldn't send messages very far.

Experience with Sound

Alexander Graham Bell was very interested in sound. His mother was deaf. His father taught deaf people how to speak. Bell also worked with deaf people. He thought a lot about speech and sound. He wanted to build something that could send sound electronically.

Previous Invention

In the late 1800s, the telegraph was the fastest way to communicate. Messages were sent along a wire using electricity. They were sent in code, then translated at their destinations. It was a slow process. At this time, people were traveling more. They wanted to talk to each other more quickly. The telegraph needed to be replaced.

Competition

Another inventor, Thomas Edison, was already well-known for his inventions. His work improved the telegraph. For years, Edison and Bell were both trying to find a way to transmit the sound of a human voice. They were competing to invent the telephone.

What Happened Next

Bell and Watson continued to work on their telephone for weeks after the first phone call worked. They made changes to the design. These changes improved the quality of the sound. Two months after his first phone call, Bell went to the Centennial Exposition in Philadelphia, Pennsylvania. Many famous scientists were there. They thought his invention was amazing.

However, other people did not like the new device. The telephone confused some people. It made them uncomfortable. People called Bell a liar. They accused him of using witchcraft. For several years, Bell and Watson showed many people the telephone. They explained how it worked. Slowly, people began to change their minds.

In April 1877, the first telephone line was installed. Charles Williams was Bell's boss at the machine shop. For years, he gave Bell money and space to work on the telephone. So Bell decided to install a telephone line for Williams. The line ran between Williams's office and his home. It was 3 miles (5 kilometers) long. Williams's telephone was very successful. More and more people wanted to get a phone of their own. Williams started building more phones. His company made 25 phones per day, and rented them to people. Soon, they spread across the United States.

In 1884, dozens of important people watched Bell make the first call from Boston, Massachusetts, to New York City—a distance of 235 miles (378 kilometers).

DID YOU KNOW?

By August, 1877—only four months after the first telephone line was installed—778 phone lines were working.

Ripple Effects

A single event, no matter how big or small it may seem at the time, can have a big impact on the future. The creation of the first telephone changed the world in a big way.

AT&T

Many new companies had to be formed to handle the new telephone lines. One of the first was the American Telephone and Telegraph Company. It was started in 1885. Today, the company is known as AT&T, and is one of the largest phone companies in the world.

Cross-Country

In 1915, AT&T built the first telephone line across the US. It reached from New York to San Francisco. Alexander Graham Bell and Thomas A. Watson made the first phone call across the country.

A Fact of Life

Today, phones are everywhere. Most people carry cell phones around in their pockets. Houses and apartments often come with telephone lines. People expect to always have access to a phone. It is hard to imagine a world without phones.

Emergency Contact

Before phones, it was hard to contact the police. Someone had to go to a police station. But even once phones were common, it was still difficult. In 1968, the Federal Communications Commission decided they needed an emergency phone number that would work everywhere in the US. They chose the number 9-1-1.

DID YOU KNOW?

The first phone call to cross the Atlantic Ocean was made on January 7, 1927. It was between London and New York City.

Early **switchboard** operators had to be at least 5 feet (1.5 meters) tall and have long arms. Otherwise, they couldn't reach all the controls.

EMMA NUTT

When people wanted to make a call on early telephones, they had to talk to an operator first. These operators were young men. They were often rude and unprofessional. Customers complained. So, Alexander Graham Bell hired Emma Nutt. Nutt was skilled, patient, and polite. She spoke with confidence and grace. Soon, all telephone operators were women. They often worked 60 hours a week, but they made very little money. In 1919, they went **on strike** and won a pay raise.

A Changing World

The telephone was a huge change from writing letters and sending telegraphs. It took time for people to get used to it. Bell, Watson, and their friends started the Bell Telephone Company. They worked hard to improve the technology. Soon, many businesses had access to a telephone line. It would be many more years before the general public also had access. However, by the 1960s, there was a telephone in almost every home in the United States.

Today's telephones have changed a lot from Bell's. Now, phones can access the internet. They can take pictures and videos, and send text messages. Not only can people talk to each other using phones, but they can access information almost instantly.

When Bell first spoke into his telephone, he couldn't have imagined how much his invention would change the world. Telephones helped businesses work faster and grow bigger. They allowed people to call for help and get a response quickly. Phones opened up many new job opportunities. They also brought people closer together, connecting people all over the United States and the world.

switchboard: a system that connected someone making a telephone call with the person they were trying to reach

strike: a period of time when people stop working in order to force their employer to agree to their demands

DID YOU KNOW?

Alexander Graham Bell thought people should answer the phone with "Ahoy!" Thomas Edison encouraged people to say "Hello!" instead.

THE FIRST FIRESIDE CHAT

March 12, 1933

It is a cold evening in late winter. Families gather in the warmest part of the house: the living room, near the fireplace. It is a hard time for many Americans. Business is bad, and lots of people have lost their jobs. They have very little money. This time period is known as the Great Depression (1929–1939).

Tonight, people aren't talking about money. They are talking about the new president: Franklin D. Roosevelt. They are hoping he can turn the **economy** around and bring back jobs. They want Roosevelt to save them and the country. Tonight, he is going to talk to the people.

Everyone is quiet as they turn on the radio. The room fills with the soothing voice of the president. "I want to talk for a few minutes with the people of the United States about banking," he says. He then explains what went wrong and what the government is doing to help, in a way that everyone can understand.

This is the first time a president has shared information with the people in such an **amiable** way. This is the first "fireside chat."

President Roosevelt sat at a desk when he gave fireside chats, surrounded by microphones and wires.

economy: the exchange of money for products and services in a particular country or area

amiable: easy to like

DID YOU KNOW?
At the time of the first fireside chat, a radio cost around $10, which would be about $185 today.

How and Why

The creation and use of new technology is a process. Many different people, events, and ideas come together when technology is used in new ways. Take a moment to explore some of the things that caused Roosevelt to begin broadcasting his historic fireside chats.

The Great Depression

In 1929, the US economy fell. The stock market crashed. Banks closed. More than $25 billion of the American people's money was lost. That would be more than $300 billion today. Up to 30 percent of working people lost their jobs. This was the start of the Great Depression.

Bank Runs

When a bank closed, customers lost all the money they had in it. Everyone was afraid of losing their money. They went to the banks and withdrew all of their cash. These "bank runs" hurt the struggling banks even more. By 1933, almost half of all the banks in the United States had closed.

Broadcasting Boom

The 1920s and early 1930s saw a big increase in radio broadcasting. By 1933, more than 60 percent of homes had a radio. People were able to listen to the news, weather reports, and sports updates. They also listened to music, short stories, educational lectures, and kids' shows. The radio provided low-cost entertainment for struggling families.

A New President

A presidential election was held in 1932. Franklin D. Roosevelt, the governor of New York, ran against Herbert Hoover, who was president at the time. Roosevelt said it was the government's job to fix the economy and give people back their jobs. On election day, he won 42 states. Hoover won six. Roosevelt became the 32nd president of the United States.

President Roosevelt often joked about the name "fireside chats." He thought it was funny because he often gave them on days when it was too warm to sit by a fire.

DID YOU KNOW?
Radios send signals in two ways. One is called FM and the other is called AM.

What Happened Next

More than 60 million people, almost half of the US population, listened to the first fireside chat. After Roosevelt explained things to the people, they were less afraid. The bank runs stopped. People started to put their money back into the banks. The banking crisis soon ended.

Roosevelt saw that his broadcast had helped. He continued talking to the people. He had 30 fireside chats between 1933 and 1944. He talked listeners through the end of the Great Depression in 1939, the attack on Pearl Harbor in 1941, and World War II (1939–1945). When a fireside chat was on the air, everyone stopped to listen. Workers put down their tools. Children stopped playing. Cab drivers pulled to the side of the road. Everyone listened together.

Before the fireside chats, newspapers often had a big impact through what they wrote. News articles were often negative. However, the radio let Roosevelt talk directly to the people. He explained his plans and policies so everyone could understand. This made people trust him. They were inspired. People had a new sense of courage and confidence.

Roosevelt shared important information during his fireside chats. This knowledge helped the people of the United States get through some very difficult times.

Ripple Effects

A single event, no matter how big or small it may seem at the time, can have a big impact on the future. The radio broadcasts of Roosevelt's fireside chats had many far-reaching effects.

Letters from the People

During his fireside chats, Roosevelt encouraged people to write to him. He started getting almost 8,000 letters a day—more than any other president in history up to that point. Today, the president usually receives about 10,000 letters and emails each day.

Debates

In 1960, the **debates** between John F. Kennedy and Richard Nixon were the first to be shown on television. TV made politics even more accessible to the country. Today, debates between politicians are shown live, on television or the internet.

Twitter

Barack Obama was the first president to use the social networking site Twitter. On May 18, 2015, he posted his first tweet. Twitter quickly became an important way for the president to reach the people. President Obama wanted the people to be able to participate in their government. Twitter is a fast and easy way to reach millions of people.

C-SPAN

In 1979, Brian Lamb founded the Cable-Satellite Public Affairs Network, or C-SPAN. It showed live footage of the House of Representatives on TV. For the first time, people could watch as the government made important decisions. Today, C-SPAN has three channels, covering all branches of government.

debate: an organized discussion where people argue their opinions on certain topics

A Tradition of Communication

The radio brought the president's voice into people's homes. Soon after, the television showed his picture, too. Roosevelt was the first president to be shown on TV, in 1939.

People began gathering around their TVs instead of their radios. President Ronald Reagan (1981–1989) was a well-known actor on television and in films. In 2017, almost 31 million people tuned in to the **inauguration** of President Donald Trump. Before entering politics, Trump was known for his appearances on reality TV shows.

Today, people can also take their communication on the road with **podcasts** and videos on their phones and laptops. President Barack Obama (2009–2017) made videos on YouTube and talked to young people on social networking sites. One of President Obama's most popular videos had almost 50 million views.

The president is accessible now in ways that people who listened to the fireside chats could never have dreamed. But the president's accessibility serves the same purpose: to bring information to the people.

podcast: a voice recording made available on the internet, usually as part of a series

inauguration: a formal ceremony to introduce an elected official into their new position

President Jimmy Carter held a fireside chat in 1977. Instead of being a radio broadcast, it was aired on television.

THE NEW DEAL

When Franklin D. Roosevelt became the president, the country was in the Great Depression. Money was worth almost nothing. Many people didn't have jobs. President Roosevelt promised to change that. He called his plan the "New Deal." He began working on this plan in the first three months that he was president. The New Deal worked. Many pieces of the New Deal still exist today, like the ideas of minimum wage, and disability insurance for people who can't work.

VIDEO GAME ADVANCEMENT

February, 1978

You are the last defense between the Earth and an army of invaders. Aliens hover above you, then inch closer and closer. They shoot at you while you dodge and fire back at them, taking them out one by one. Can you defeat them in time to save the Earth?

No, this is not a real alien attack. It is 1978, and this is the most popular video game in Japan. Toshihiro Nishikado spent years creating an exciting new video game—one unlike anything people had seen before. The game is called *Space Invaders*. It is a two-dimensional top-down shooter game. In it, the player is located at the bottom of the screen. They must defend Earth from an army of aliens attacking from the top.

Most of the video games that came before *Space Invaders* were very simple and similar to each other. But now, *Space Invaders* offers something new.

Two years later, in 1980, *Space Invaders* arrives in the United States. It is just as successful as it was in Japan. **Arcades** buy as many copies of the game as they can get. People wait in lines for hours to play. They don't know this at the time, but *Space Invaders* is about to change the future of video games.

Studies have shown that adults spend just as much time playing video games as kids, and many families play together.

arcade: an indoor area containing coin-operated video games

DID YOU KNOW?

The first-ever video game was released in 1971. It was called *Computer Space*. It was similar to *Space Invaders*. But it was difficult to learn. Most people lost interest.

How and Why

The creation and use of new technology is a process. Many different people, events, and ideas come together when new technology is needed. Below are some of the things that led to the invention and success of *Space Invaders*.

The First Console

Televisions were becoming more common and more popular. People began to wonder what else they could do with a television screen. In the 1960s, people started to design electronic games. A man named Ralph Baer built the first gaming console. The console was a small box with controls like those at an arcade.

Pong

Pong was the first arcade video game. It came out in 1972. *Pong* was an electronic version of table tennis. In 1974 it was released as a home game, called *Home Pong*. It started the video game trend.

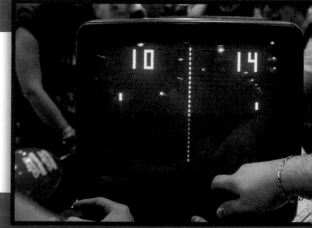

Losing Interest

Although people loved *Pong*, they got used to it quickly, and it became less popular. Many of the new games that were released after *Pong* weren't original. Most of them were different versions of *Pong*. The video game industry began to die out. Atari, who had made *Pong*, was looking for something new. If their next game succeeded, the company would survive.

Sci-Fi Fascination

Close Encounters of the Third Kind and *Star Wars* both came out in 1977. These two science-fiction films became very popular. Suddenly, science fiction was everywhere. People wanted more sci-fi. *Space Invaders* was exactly what they were looking for.

What Happened Next

Space Invaders was an instant hit. Before video games became popular, arcades had been mostly filled with **pinball** machines. Now, people were showing up at arcades to play *Space Invaders*.

The game was unlike any other. *Space Invaders* told a story. The player was protecting Earth from aliens. It also introduced new ideas, like cutscenes. These are scenes that tell a story after each level. Players also had multiple lives. If they died, the game wasn't over. They had another chance. Music was an important part of the game. As the player killed more aliens, the music got faster. The aliens also started to move faster.

Other companies rushed to create more video games like *Space Invaders*. Many games that came out after *Space Invaders* were almost exactly the same. Atari was doing well with the success of *Space Invaders*. They hired more designers to come up with new ideas. Soon companies like Nintendo started designing new games as well.

pinball: a game in which the player tries to control a ball with a set of levers, and points are scored by hitting targets

There were more than 10,000 contestants in the 1980 National Space Invaders Championships. The winner was 14-year-old Bill Heineman, who went on to create video games.

DID YOU KNOW?
Space Invaders was the first video game that let players save their high scores.

Ripple Effects

A single event, no matter how big or small it may seem at the time, can have a big impact on the future. The popularity of *Space Invaders* influenced the video game world for years to come.

A Popular Trend

Space Invaders was the first shooter game that became popular. People really liked the science-fiction story behind *Space Invaders*. Games about aliens became popular. People also began to enjoy games with a story and characters, rather than sports-based games like *Pong*.

Making Games Accessible

Before *Space Invaders*, not many people could play video games in their homes. Most people went to arcades. But the lines at arcades were often too long and people wanted to play any time they wanted. A month after *Space Invaders* came out, Atari released the Atari 2600 home console. It sold about 400,000 units that same year.

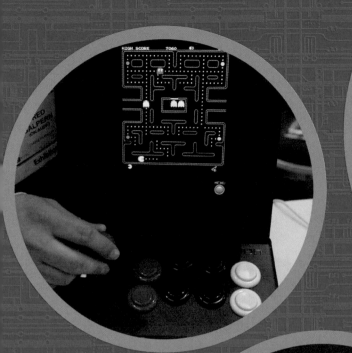

The Adventures Continue

Halo 5: Guardians is part of a series of games about defending earth from an alien invasion. This game is made by Xbox. Between 2001 and 2015, *Halo* made more than $5 billion dollars. Without Atari and *Space Invaders*, Xbox and *Halo* may have never existed.

Pac-Man

Pac-Man came out just two years after *Space Invaders*. Like Space Invaders, there was a story behind this game. In *Pac-Man*, the main character tries to escape a maze without getting caught by ghosts. By 1982, *Pac-Man* had sold 14,000 units. By 1999, the game had made $2.5 billion.

People spend an average of six hours a week playing video games. About half of that time is spent playing with other people.

SPACE INVADERS TODAY

As technology has changed, *Space Invaders* has been updated and re-released. Now, it can be played on almost any console. Versions of it are free on the internet. The images of the original *Space Invaders* can be found everywhere. They're on shirts, mugs, keychains, and even ice cube trays.

Gaming Legacy

In 1978, *Space Invaders* pushed the limits of technology. The game's creator even had to build a special computer to play the game. At the time, the game couldn't run on normal computers. None of them were fast enough. They didn't have the power that *Space Invaders* needed.

The story-telling technology that *Space Invaders* introduced can still be seen in today's video games. For example, many puzzle games speed up as you move through the levels. Sometimes in strategy games the music changes when the player is close to losing. *Space Invaders* did those things first.

When Atari launched *Space Invaders*, it was just the beginning of video games' rise to popularity. Today, video games are everywhere, including on phones. In 2016, the video game industry made more than $91 billion. More than 155 million people play video games in the US. It all started with a tiny space ship trying to defend Earth from an alien invasion.

DID YOU KNOW?
The aliens in *Space Invaders* were designed to look similar to sea creatures, like squids and crabs.

The Future of Smartphones

June 29, 2007

Thousands of people stand on sidewalks across the United States. They've been waiting in lines for hours. The stores are about to open. Finally, customers are going to be able to buy Apple's newest product, the iPhone. The doors open and people file in to pick up their new phones. The box is smooth and white. People open the packaging and there, in their hands, is the **smartphone** of the future.

The phone isn't big or colorful. It has a simple design. The screen is only 3.5 inches (8.9 centimeters). It is about half an inch thick.

Suddenly, people are connected to the internet almost all the time. There's always a high-definition camera in their pocket. The world is at their fingertips. It's easy to use. All people have to do is touch the screen. They can use their fingers to zoom in on pictures or websites. Nobody has ever seen a phone like this.

smartphone: a cell phone that can send and receive email, access the internet, and take photos

More than 90 million people in the United States use an iPhone. That's almost one out of every three people.

DID YOU KNOW?
In the first 30 hours of sales, Apple sold 270,000 of the first iPhones.

How and Why

The creation and use of new technology is a process. Many different people, events, and ideas come together when new technology is needed. Take a moment to discover some of the things that led to the success of the iPhone.

The First Smartphone

In the 1990s, computers the size of phones, called personal digital assistants (PDAs) were being used alongside cell phones. Nokia launched the first smartphone in 1996. This combined a PDA and a phone. It was big and expensive. It cost about $800, and not many people bought it.

The iPod

The CEO of Apple, Steve Jobs, wanted to change the music industry. At this time, most people listened to music on CDs. But he knew that there were better ways to store and listen to songs. In 2001 Apple released the first iPod. It could hold up to 1,000 songs, fit in your pocket, and was easy to use.

Touchscreens

Apple had been building touchscreens for a while. They had been working on tablet computers. These are computers that don't have a mouse. Instead, they have touchscreens. But Jobs wanted to take it even further. He wanted to build touchscreen phones.

A Big Announcement

At the 2007 Macworld conference in San Francisco, Apple took over the building for a week. There, on January 9, Steve Jobs announced the iPhone. He showed off a cell phone that had one button and a large touchscreen. It could also connect to the internet and play music.

What Happened Next

The iPhone was a big success. It was the fastest-selling Apple product at the time. People loved it. On September 10, 2007, Apple announced that they'd sold their millionth phone. This was only 74 days after it was released.

It was the first fully touchscreen device. It also provided easy internet access. People could load any website they wanted. They could receive and send email. The phone even worked as a **GPS**. The phone acted like many tools in one.

Other companies realized that Apple was changing the cell phone industry. Samsung and Google started building touchscreen phones, too. Many copied the way the iPhone looked. The new phones were thin and didn't have very many buttons. Some of these phones started to sell very well. By the end of 2008, Apple had sold more than 11 million iPhones. They had also changed how people connected to the world.

GPS: a device that uses satellites to tell you your location and give you directions

Apple made more than $53 billion on iPhone sales in 2016. That's enough money to give every person in the United States $165.

DID YOU KNOW?
In total, the first generation of iPhones sold just over six million phones.

Ripple Effects

A single event, no matter how big or small it may seem at the time, can have a big impact on the future. The iPhone changed the way we think of phones, and helped shape the future of communication.

From Phones to Tablets

Before the iPhone, tablet computers weren't popular. But then the iPhone came out. People started to love using a touchscreen. In 2010, Apple decided to release a tablet. They called it the iPad. Many other companies started to build tablets, too.

Applications

The iPhone doesn't just make money for Apple. Lots of other businesses are connected to it. Many people build applications, called "apps," that are used on iPhones. Companies make billions of dollars building and selling apps. Apple even has a saying about it. "There's an app for that!"

Staying Connected

People are now easier to call, text, or email. Everyone is connected. Today, many people don't have to work in an office. They can work anywhere when they have internet and email on their phone. This also means people can work any time. In 2016, around 30 percent of employed people "telecommuted"—they did some or all of their work from home.

Growing Popularity

The iPhone changed how people interact with technology. The design was simple and the touchscreen was easy to use. One of the biggest groups buying iPads in 2015 were people more than 65 years old.

DID YOU KNOW?
There are more than 2.2 billion apps available on the App Store.

iPhones are made mostly of glass, metal, and plastic. They also contain small amounts of rare metals, such as neodymium, terbium, and gadolinium.

THE FIRST CELL PHONE

Cell phones are a lot older than people think. The first call from a cell phone was made in 1973. The phone itself was huge. It was 11 inches (28 centimeters) tall and weighed 2.5 pounds (1.1 kilograms). It was built by Motorola. But this was just a prototype, or a test phone. It could only be used for 30 minutes before the battery died. It could store only 30 phone numbers. Cell phones weren't sold to the public until 10 years later, in 1983.

The Future is Calling

The iPhone pushed cell phone and touchscreen technology into the future. It also caused many social ripple effects. Parents can see where kids are by tracking their phones. People can easily send an email or answer a work call while on vacation. Finding the answer to almost any question is easier than ever.

Apple and other companies push technology forward with the iPhone and similar products. Today, the world moves faster than ever. People want to be able to access information quickly, without waiting. Now, people can even ask their iPhones questions by saying, "Hey Siri." Without even touching their phones, people can check the weather or the score of a baseball game.

By 2017, Apple had sold more than one billion iPhones. They also launched the Apple Watch, another smart device, in 2015. What will be next?

DID YOU KNOW?
In 2007, *Time Magazine* named Apple's iPhone the "invention of the year."

Quiz

1 In the 1800s, before the telephone was invented, what was the fastest way to communicate?

The telegraph

2 In what year was the first telephone line installed?

1877

3 How many people listened to the first fireside chat?

More than 60 million

4 Who was the first president to be shown on TV?

Franklin D. Roosevelt

5 The first arcade video game was released in 1972. What was it called?

Pong

6 How much money did the video game industry make in 2016?

More than $91 billion

7 In what year did the company Nokia launch the first smartphone?

1996

8 After the iPhone was first released, how long did it take Apple to sell one million iPhones?

74 days

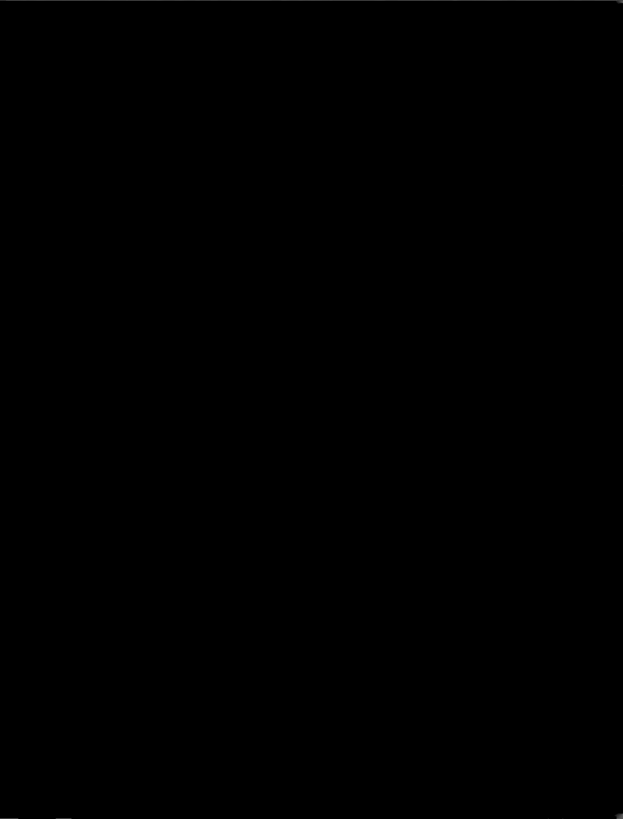

Index

Read More

Bader, Bonnie. *Who Was Alexander Graham Bell?* New York, NY: Grosset & Dunlap, 2013.

Spilsbury, Louise. *Alexander Graham Bell and the Telephone.* Inventions That Changed the World. New York, NY: PowerKids Press, 2016.

Frith, Margaret. *Who Was Franklin Roosevelt?* New York, NY: Grosset & Dunlap, 2010.

Kudlinski, Kathleen V. *Franklin Delano Roosevelt: Champion of Freedom.* Childhood of Famous Americans. New York, NY: Aladdin, 2003.

Hansen, Dustin. *Game On! Video Game History from Pong to Pac-Man to Mario, Minecraft, and Beyond.* New York, NY: Feiwel & Friends, 2016.

Paris, David, and Stephanie Herweck Paris. *History of Video Games.* TIME FOR KIDS® Nonfiction Readers. Huntington Beach, CA: Teacher Created Materials, 2016.

Mangor, Jodie. *Inventing the Cell Phone.* Spark of Invention. Mankato, MN: Momentum, 2016.

Pollack, Pam, and Meg Belviso. *Who Was Steve Jobs?* New York, NY: Grosset & Dunlap, 2012.